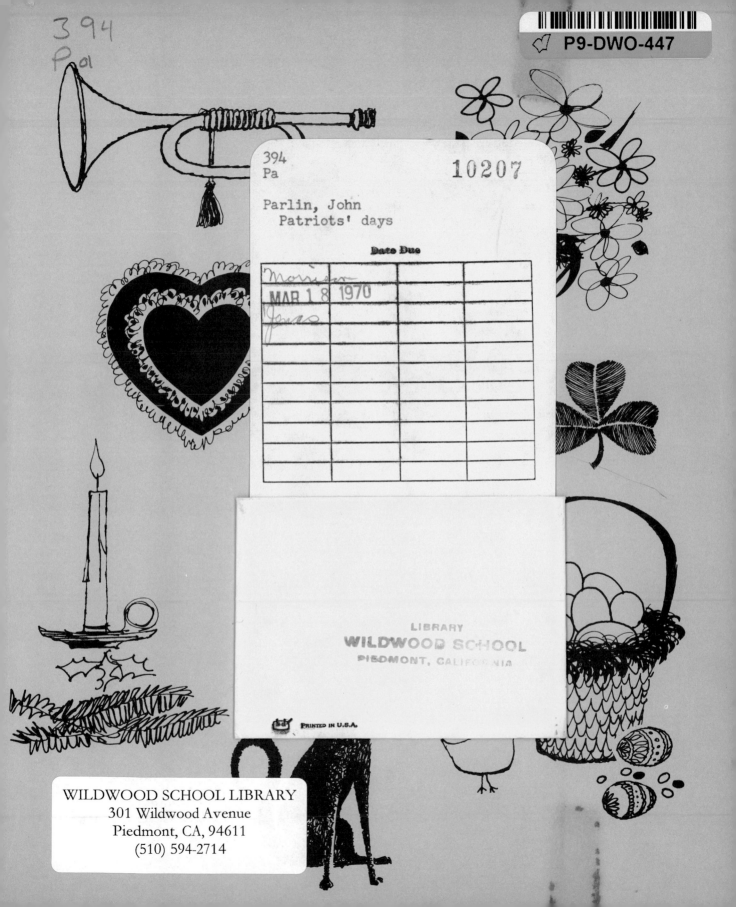

A HOLIDAY BOOK

Patriots' Days

BY JOHN PARLIN

ILLUSTRATED BY ROBERT DOREMUS

GARRARD PUBLISHING COMPANY
CHAMPAIGN, ILLINOIS

For Jane K. Valleau

The author and publisher are grateful to Alfred Kreymborg
for permission to quote from his poem,
"The Lincoln Penny"

Holiday Books are edited under
the educational supervision of

Charles E. Johnson, Ed.D.
Associate Professor of Education
University of Illinois

Published in Champaign, Illinois, by Garrard Publishing Company
Manufactured in the United States of America

Library of Congress Catalog Card Number: 64-17334

Contents

1
Washington's Birthday

George Washington was the first President of the United States. His birthday has been celebrated longer than that of any other American patriot.

School and store windows are often decorated with paper cherries and hatchets for Washington's Birthday. That's because of the famous story about Washington chopping a cherry tree when he was a boy.

This story appeared in a book written in 1800 by Parson Mason Weems.

In Weems' story George went up to his father one day and asked, "Father, do I ever tell lies?"

"No, George," his father answered. "You always tell the truth. I am thankful for that."

A few days later George had his sixth birthday. His father gave him a shiny new hatchet for a present. George ran into the garden to try it out.

There was a beautiful cherry tree in the garden. It was Mr. Washington's favorite tree, but George forgot all about that. He swung his hatchet. The sharp edge bit deeply into the wood.

Suddenly, George realized that the tree would die. He hoped his father would not notice.

6

The next morning Mr. Washington went into the garden and saw what George had done.

"That was the prettiest tree in the garden," he said angrily. "I'd like to get my hands on the rascal who chopped it."

Just then George appeared. He was holding his hatchet.

"George!" his father called. "Do you know who chopped my beautiful cherry tree?"

For a few seconds George was silent. He was afraid he would be punished if he told the truth. But he knew it was wrong to lie.

"George," his father began again, "I asked you if you knew who killed . . ."

"Oh, Father!" George cried. "I cannot tell a lie. I did it with my hatchet."

George thought he would be punished. Instead his father put his arms around him.

"Son," he said gently, "I don't care if you did kill the tree. You have paid me for it a thousand times by telling the truth."

The story is probably just a legend. George was a good boy, but he wasn't perfect all the time.

People love the story, however. It is often told at birthday celebrations in honor of Washington. Sometimes schools decorate their windows with paper hatchets and cherry trees. Restaurants serve cherry pie.

Today we celebrate Washington's Birthday on February 22. But when George Washington was a boy his birthday came on February 11.

There is a simple explanation for this. Washington was born at Wakefield, Virginia, in 1732. At that time America used a different calendar from the one we use today. Most places in America started using a new calendar when Washington was a young man. Eleven days were added to each old date. That made Washington's birthday fall on February 22.

When Washington was born America belonged to England and celebrated the birthday of the English king. People built bonfires, fired cannons and rang bells.

When America declared her independence in 1776, people stopped celebrating the king's birthday.

Washington was a grown man then. He was head of the American Army.

In February, 1778, Washington and his army were at Valley Forge, Pennsylvania. It was terribly cold. Many soldiers were dressed in rags and were almost starving. But on Washington's birthday an army band marched through the snow to his headquarters and played for him.

The men admired Washington's courage and military leadership. They knew he would do everything he could to lead them to victory.

After the long war was won a new government was set up. The American colonies were now the United States. Everyone knew whom they wanted for

President—Washington. He served for two terms and made the new government strong and successful.

When Washington became President the capital was in New York. Later it was moved to Philadelphia.

Philadelphia celebrated the President's birthday in a big way. Schools closed and nearly everybody had a holiday. Flags flew from buildings and soldiers paraded.

All day people came to Washington's

home to wish him a happy birthday. His wife, Martha, gave them cake and punch.

That night the Washingtons were invited to a party in their honor. They went in a beautiful coach drawn by six horses.

A large crowd was waiting to see Washington arrive. People cheered when he got out of his coach. Gold buttons gleamed on his velvet coat. An ostrich plume waved from his cocked hat and a sword flashed at his side.

People in other parts of the country celebrated Washington's birthday too. While he was still President the custom spread throughout the nation. It continued even after his years as President ended. People celebrated much as they had for the king. But now they were honoring a great American. Proudly, Americans called Washington the "Father of his country."

2
America Celebrates

When Washington left the Presidency he returned to his home, Mount Vernon. This was a beautiful plantation on the banks of the Potomac River in Virginia.

In 1799, Washington attended two birthday parties. Alexandria, a city near Mount Vernon, still used the old calendar. The people there celebrated Washington's Birthday on February 11.

Washington rode into Alexandria shortly before noon. Many soldiers on horseback rode through the streets with him.

To entertain Washington the soldiers had a make-believe war. Soldiers on ships in the river "attacked" Alexandria. The Alexandria soldiers fought back. Washington cheered when the Alexandria soldiers "captured" the ships.

That evening there was a big party in Alexandria. Washington's friends came and danced until after midnight.

There was another celebration at Mount Vernon on February 22. Washington's granddaughter, Nelly Custis, picked his birthday for her wedding day.

Washington ordered a new uniform with gold decorations for the wedding. The tailor did not finish it in time. So Washington dressed in an old uniform that he had worn in the Revolution.

Nelly wore a beautiful wedding dress and some white plumes from Paris. She and her fiancé, Lawrence Lewis, were married by candlelight.

This was Washington's last birthday. He died the next December.

The country mourned him. One of his old soldiers said Washington was *"First in war, first in peace, and first in the hearts of his countrymen."*

Washington's body was placed in a tomb at Mount Vernon. Two years later Martha Washington died. Her body was put in the tomb with her husband.

After Washington's death, people still honored him on his birthday. February 22 became an annual holiday, just like the Fourth of July.

The biggest celebration of all was in 1932, the 200th anniversary of George Washington's birth. A 200th anniversary is called a bicentennial.

When Washington was alive he loved to plant trees. He dug up dogwood, holly and redbud in the forests near Mount Vernon and planted them around the house. He asked friends in New England and Europe to send him rare trees.

17

Because Washington had loved trees the people decided to celebrate his bicentennial by planting millions of trees. These trees would be "living memorials" to George Washington.

President Herbert Hoover planted an elm on the White House lawn. Millions of boys and girls planted living memorials to Washington. State governors planted trees too.

Thousands of Boy Scouts went to Valley Forge, Pennsylvania, on February 22 that year. Another famous general spoke to the Scouts. He told them that Washington was an *"ideal American citizen."*

During the bicentennial year the Post Office department issued twelve different stamps in Washington's honor.

A writer and actor named George M. Cohan wrote a Washington's Birthday song. It ends with these lines:

"First in War, First in Peace,
First in the hearts of his countrymen,
That is the story of Washington,
That is the glory of Washington,
His spirit is here, his spirit is here,
He's standing, commanding above,
In word and deed we follow the lead
Of the Father of the land we love."

3
Mount Vernon and the Washington Monument

After Washington's death thousands of people wanted to see his home and tomb. They flocked to Mount Vernon. The family did not have much privacy.

Mount Vernon passed from one member of the Washington family to another. The last relative to live there was John Augustine Washington. He did not have enough money to keep Mount Vernon in good repair. Weeds grew everywhere and the house needed painting.

John Washington tried to get the federal government to buy Mount Vernon for all Americans. The government refused. He offered to sell it to Virginia. Virginia would not buy it.

Luckily something happened that was to save Mount Vernon for all time.

In the middle of the nineteenth century there were many steamboats on the Potomac River. As the boats neared Mount Vernon they would slow down and toll their bells in honor of Washington.

One night an old lady was on one of these boats traveling on the Potomac. She saw Mount Vernon bathed in the moonlight. It was a sad sight. Even in the moonlight it looked shabby and rundown.

The old lady was upset when she saw what had happened to Washington's home. She wrote to her daughter about it.

Her daughter, Ann Cunningham, lived in South Carolina. When Ann read her mother's letter she decided to try to save Mount Vernon. She formed an organization which was called the Mount Vernon Ladies' Association of the Union.

Miss Cunningham learned that it would cost $200,000 to buy Mount Vernon. She was a determined woman. She went to work to raise the money.

A statesman from Massachusetts named Edward Everett helped her. He made speeches in many cities asking people to give money to save Mount Vernon. He gave a great deal of money himself.

School children saved their pennies for Mount Vernon. A boy in Louisiana raised so much money that he earned a new nickname. He was called the "Little Knight of Mount Vernon."

A famous writer sent a check for $500. The writer was Washington Irving. He was named for George Washington.

Newspapers printed an old story about Washington Irving. When he was five years old he was walking along a street in New York City with his nurse. The nurse saw a large crowd standing outside a building.

"What are all you people doing?" she asked.

"Waiting to see George Washington come out," a man said.

The nurse marched little Washington Irving inside the building. She went up to George Washington and said, "Here's a boy who is named after you."

George Washington smiled. He put his hands on the boy's head.

When he was a grown man Washington

Irving said, *"I can still feel that hand upon my head."*

People who read about the meeting between Washington Irving and George Washington liked the story. They sent money to Miss Cunningham.

At last she had enough money to buy Mount Vernon. On February 22, 1860, John Washington moved out of his house and the Mount Vernon Ladies' Association moved in. It was a happy Washington's Birthday for America.

The next year, however, was a sad one. The Civil War broke out between the North and the South.

On February 22, 1861, a strange celebration took place in the harbor of Charleston, South Carolina. The Southern soldiers were at Castle Pinckney. Northern soldiers were a few miles away at Fort Sumter.

At sunrise the Southern soldiers fired thirteen guns in honor of Washington's Birthday. At noon the cannon at Sumter boomed another salute. Washington was the father of both the North and the South.

During the war soldiers often came to visit Mount Vernon. Sometimes men from both sides met at Washington's tomb. They bowed their heads in silence.

When the war was over Miss Cunningham and the Mount Vernon Ladies' Association started restoring Washington's home. They wanted it to look as it did when he lived there.

They repaired the house and fixed the lawns and gardens. They searched America for furniture and other articles that were in the house when Washington lived there.

Today Mount Vernon is always freshly painted, and the grounds are beautifully landscaped.

More than a million people visit Mount Vernon each year. Among them are thousands of children. Many of the visitors speak in hushed voices. They know they are walking where Washington walked so many years ago.

While the ladies were raising money to purchase Mount Vernon, the great Washington Monument was being built in the District of Columbia.

The Washington Monument has a long and interesting history. At the time of Washington's death Congress said that a

"marble monument" should be built in his memory. But Congress did not give any money for a monument.

In 1833, some citizens formed the Washington National Monument Society and started raising money. Work on the monument started in 1848.

As it went up, many memorial stones were placed inside the walls of the hollow shaft. These stones came from cities, states, organizations, schools and individuals.

The Pope in Rome sent a beautiful block of Italian marble. Before the marble could be placed in the monument it was stolen. It was never found.

The theft of the Pope's stone made Americans angry. People would not give any more money for the monument.

In 1854, work stopped. The unfinished monument was 153 feet high.

A few years later the Civil War started. Many people feared the monument would never be finished.

After the war Congress decided that the federal government should complete the monument. In 1880, work started again.

Finally the monument was finished. It was 555 feet, 5⅛ inches high. It was dedicated on the eve of Washington's Birthday in 1885. One hundred guns were fired as a salute to Washington.

One of the speakers said that the *"monument looks down on the scenes most loved by Washington."*

From the top you can see Alexandria where Washington went to church. You can see the Potomac River where he swam as a boy.

The Washington Monument is one of the symbols of the capital city of the

United States. Fifty American flags, one for each state, fly at its base.

Visitors to the monument can ride in the elevator to the top, but many children climb the 898 steps. At each landing they can read the memorial stones set in the walls.

The words on the Virginia stone read, *"Virginia who gave Washington to America gives this granite for his monument."*

California gave a stone of gold-bearing quartz soon after she became a state. The inscription says, *"California: Youngest Sister of the Union Brings her Golden Tribute to the Memory of its Father."*

Indiana's stone reads, *"Indiana knows no North, no South, Nothing but the Union."*

Children always have fun looking for the stones given by their native states.

4
Thomas Jefferson

Flags fly and rockets flare every Fourth of July. We are celebrating our nation's independence. We are also honoring a great patriot, Thomas Jefferson. Jefferson was the author of the Declaration of Independence which Congress adopted on July 4, 1776.

Jefferson was born on April 13, 1743, at Shadwell, Virginia. He had a brilliant mind and grew up loving books and reading.

He studied mathematics, architecture, law and science. There was little that did not interest him.

Young Jefferson represented Virginia in the new Continental Congress. Because he was such a good writer he was chosen to draft the Declaration of Independence. Jefferson's words will never be forgotten.

"We hold these truths to be self-evident, that all men are created equal, that they are endowed by their Creator with certain unalienable rights, that among these are Life, Liberty, and the pursuit of Happiness."

Jefferson was Governor of Virginia and later the third President of the United States. He worked hard to make sure that those rights, promised in the Declaration of Independence and in the Constitution, became reality.

He felt that people should be allowed to worship as they pleased. He believed that everyone should be educated so that the people could govern themselves well.

As President, Jefferson was responsible for the Louisiana Purchase. The United States bought this vast western territory from France. It almost doubled the size of the United States.

When Jefferson left the Presidency he returned to his home, Monticello. Monticello means "Little Mountain." Jefferson had designed the house, built on a Virginia hilltop. Its dome and pillars influenced the design of the White House and of the Capitol Building in Washington.

Jefferson loved Monticello. He rode horseback there. He supervised the farm work and planted new crops. He played the violin and he played with his children and grandchildren. *"All my wishes end,"* Jefferson once said, *"where I hope my days will end, at Monticello."*

Jefferson died at Monticello on the Fourth of July in 1826. He was buried in a small family cemetery. The words on his stone say:

"Here was buried
Thomas Jefferson
Author of the
Declaration of American Independence
of the Statute of Virginia for
Religious Freedom and Father of the
University of Virginia."

Jefferson had written the inscription before he died. He was most proud of these accomplishments.

Today Monticello is a museum. It was

bought by the Thomas Jefferson Memorial Foundation, a group formed on Jefferson's Birthday in 1923.

On Jefferson's 200th birthday in 1943, there was a big celebration in Washington, D. C. The beautiful Jefferson Memorial was dedicated. It is a stone temple with a statue of Jefferson inside.

Every year on Jefferson's Birthday a special program is held at his memorial. Wreaths and bouquets are piled at the foot of the statue.

Visitors admire Jefferson's wonderful words written on the wall overhead.

"I have sworn upon the altar of God eternal hostility against every form of tyranny over the mind of man."

Jefferson is one of the four American Presidents whose faces are carved on Mount Rushmore in South Dakota. The other faces carved on the mountain are those of George Washington, Abraham Lincoln, and Theodore Roosevelt. Theodore Roosevelt, the twenty-sixth President of the United States, fought for good government, conservation and the building of the Panama Canal.

The Rushmore Memorial is often called the Shrine of Democracy. It was created by the sculptor Gutzon Borglum. He chose the Presidents he thought had done the most to establish and maintain the ideals of our nation.

It was not easy to carve the giant faces on the wild mountain cliff. Borglum was helped by his son Lincoln and many workers. They hung from the mountaintop in harnesses, with cables 300 feet long. They used dynamite and drills to chip away the granite. The heads of the Presidents are 60 feet high. A man can stand in Jefferson's eye!

President Franklin D. Roosevelt dedicated the head of Jefferson in 1936. During the ceremony an airplane flew overhead. It dropped 83 small parachutes, each with a piece of granite that had been blasted from the mountain. They stood for the 83 years that Jefferson had lived.

5
Lincoln's Birthday

Abraham Lincoln was born nine years after George Washington died. The date of his birth was February 12, 1809. The place was a log cabin on a farm near Hodgenville, Kentucky.

One of Abe's best-loved books when he was a boy was the book about George Washington by Parson Weems. The story about the cherry tree was Abe's favorite.

The first time Abe read the book he borrowed it from a friend. Some rain splashed on the book and damaged it.

Abe was a poor boy. But he was determined to buy his friend a new book. He worked three days to earn the money. During his lifetime, he always paid his debts no matter how large or small. He earned the nickname "Honest Abe."

Young Abe Lincoln helped his father with the farm work. As he grew older he chopped down trees to clear the land. He split logs to make rail fences. When Lincoln ran for President, he was called "The Railsplitter." Fence rails are often used for Lincoln's Birthday decorations.

Lincoln had a great sense of humor. He liked to tell funny stories. Children ran to meet him when he came down the street. Perhaps he would tell them a story about things he did when he was a boy.

Lincoln usually wore a tall black hat called a "stovepipe hat." He kept letters and notes in the inside band. Stovepipe hats are also used as decorations on Lincoln's Birthday.

The Civil War was fought while Lincoln was President. It was a long, hard war. Many people criticized Lincoln. His reply was, *"I do the best I can, the very best I can; and I mean to keep doing it to the end."*

Lincoln paced his room at night worrying about the deaths on the battlefields. His face was etched with sadness. He hated war, yet he knew the fighting must go on.

The United States must not be divided.

The biggest battle of the Civil War was fought at Gettysburg, Pennsylvania. Thousands of brave soldiers on both sides were killed. The battle ended in a victory for the North.

A few months after the battle Lincoln went to Gettysburg. Part of the battlefield was dedicated as a national cemetery.

The main speaker was Edward Everett. He was the man who helped save Mount Vernon. Everett spoke for about two hours.

Then Abraham Lincoln stood up. He spoke for only three minutes, but the words he said will live forever.

He closed his Gettysburg Address by saying . . . *"that this nation, under God, shall have a new birth of freedom, and that government of the people, by the people, for the people shall not perish from the earth."*

Lincoln led the North to victory in the Civil War. He saved the Union and freed the slaves.

Just as the war ended Lincoln was shot and killed. The first February 12 after his death was a day of mourning in the North. Flags flew at half-mast. In the South people paid no attention to Lincoln's Birthday.

As the years went by Lincoln's Birthday began to be observed in various ways in the northern states. Schools had special assemblies.

The biggest celebration was in 1909. That was the 100th anniversary of Lincoln's birth. For the first time many places in the South observed Lincoln's Birthday.

Theodore Roosevelt was President in 1909. He went to Hodgenville, Kentucky, on February 12. Roosevelt laid the corner-stone for a memorial to be built where Lincoln was born.

There is a log cabin inside of this memorial. When the memorial was built people thought the log cabin was the one in which Lincoln was born. Now we are not sure it is the same one. But we know it is similar to Lincoln's first home.

At Gettysburg, Pennsylvania, Lincoln's famous address was read once more from the battlefield.

"The world will little note nor long remember what we say here," Lincoln had said in his address. How wrong he was! The world probably will never forget what he said at Gettysburg.

Lincoln had made another famous speech at Cooper Union in New York City. On his 100th birthday a tablet was dedicated at Cooper Union. These words from his speech are on the tablet:

"Let us have faith that right makes might, and in that faith let us to the end dare to do our duty as we understand it."

That night in New York City the Republicans had a dinner honoring Lincoln. Lincoln had been the first Republican President. A guest at the dinner was a Negro who had been a slave: His name was Booker T. Washington. He was now a famous teacher and leader of his people.

Booker T. Washington made a speech. He told the Republicans that his mother had prayed that Lincoln would free the slaves. He said that in celebrating Lincoln's Birthday they were celebrating the answer to his mother's prayer.

Another Negro leader, Robert R. Moton, spoke when the Lincoln Memorial in Washington was dedicated in 1922. He told of the part American Negroes had played in building the nation.

The Lincoln Memorial is a large hall

made of white Colorado marble. The hall is surrounded by marble columns. The names of the 36 states that made up the United States when Lincoln died are engraved above the columns.

The inside of the hall is made of Indiana limestone and Alabama and Tennessee marble. Seated in a stone chair in the center of the hall is a giant statue of Lincoln. His face is thoughtful and kind, and beautifully carved. On the wall behind the statue appear these words:

"In this temple as in the hearts of the people for whom he saved the Union the memory of Abraham Lincoln is enshrined forever."

Two of Lincoln's famous speeches appear on the other walls. They are the Gettysburg Address and the Second Inaugural Address.

On every Lincoln's Birthday a band

plays at the Lincoln Memorial. Flowers are sent by patriotic organizations.

On one Lincoln's Birthday a Negro boy, on behalf of his school, laid some flowers by Lincoln's statue. He looked up at Lincoln's face and said, "Thank you, Mr. Lincoln."

A Lincoln memorial is probably in your pocket right now. Since Lincoln's 100th Birthday in 1909, his face has been on every penny issued by the Mint. And since 1959, the Lincoln Memorial has appeared on the back of all new pennies.

A poem called *The Lincoln Penny* was written in honor of Lincoln's Birthday in 1942. Here's the way the poem ends:

"Look at that small penny,
Hold it close to you—
And if you ever lose your way,
Abe will lead you through."

Alfred Kreymborg

6
Robert E. Lee

One hero of the Civil War who will not be forgotten is General Robert E. Lee.

Lee was a Southerner. He fought against the North. Yet he is respected today by both North and South. It is part of America's greatness that we respect all people who try to do what they think is right.

Robert E. Lee was born at Stratford, Virginia, January 19, 1807. His father, General Henry Lee, was the man who said George Washington was *"first in war, first in peace, and first in the hearts of his countrymen."*

When Lee was a young army officer he married Mary Custis. The wedding took place at Arlington Hall, the Custis family home in Virginia.

Mary's father, George Washington Parke Custis, was an adopted grandson of the first President. He had grown up at Mount Vernon. After Washington died, Custis built the Arlington mansion a short distance up the river from Mount Vernon. He brought many of Washington's personal belongings to Arlington. He entertained many patriots. Among them were Lafayette, Andrew Jackson and Sam Houston.

Mary and Robert Lee often returned to Arlington. Their children were born there. They inherited the estate when Mary's parents died.

Lee served the United States as an army officer for 30 years. He fought bravely in the Mexican War. Later he was head of the United States Military Academy at West Point.

When the Civil War broke out Lee was offered command of a Union army. Lee had to make a choice. As much as he loved the United States he could not fight against his native Virginia.

Robert E. Lee did what he thought was right. He sat down at his desk in Arlington and wrote a letter resigning from the United States Army.

During the Civil War, Lee led the Southern soldiers in Virginia. He was a great general. Often he won battles against armies much larger than his own. He always gave his soldiers credit for the victories. They loved and admired him.

Lee could not win every battle. The Northern Army grew stronger. Lee had trained many of their officers when he was at West Point. He had done a good job.

In the battle of Gettysburg, Lee suffered

his worst defeat. Afterwards he said, *"This has been my fight and upon my shoulders rests the blame."* Lee praised his soldiers. *"I never saw troops behave more magnificently."*

Finally Lee had to surrender his army. He begged his fellow Southerners to become loyal members of the Union once again.

Today Lee is honored by all Americans as a man who cared enough to fight for what he believed was right. His birthday is observed in most southern states. School children sing "Dixie" in his honor. Sometimes they draw pictures of his favorite horse, Traveller.

Every January 19, flowers are placed on Lee's tomb at Lexington, Virginia.

Throughout the year many visitors come to the Custis-Lee mansion, as Lee's Arlington home is now called. It stands on a grassy hill above the Potomac River. Its white pillars shine in the sunlight. It is a memorial to Lee and is cared for by the National Park Service.

During the Civil War, the federal government took over the Custis-Lee land and made a national cemetery at Arlington. Confederate and Union soldiers lie there together, now united forever. More than 100,000 soldiers from all our wars have now been buried at Arlington.

7
The View from Arlington

Our Presidents' birthdays have not been widely celebrated while they were alive. The two exceptions were George Washington and Franklin Delano Roosevelt.

Roosevelt was born at Hyde Park, New York, on January 30, 1882. When he was

56

39, he was crippled by polio. But that didn't keep him from becoming Governor of New York. Then, in 1933, he became President of the United States.

When he was President big balls were held all over America in his honor. They took place every year on his birthday. These "Birthday Balls" raised money for the March of Dimes. The money was used to fight polio. Now few people get this terrible disease, and the March of Dimes helps other causes.

Roosevelt was the only President to serve more than two terms. He was elected four times.

President Roosevelt called his plan the New Deal. When he became President millions of Americans were out of work. Many families had almost nothing to eat. Roosevelt tried to help the working man. He started our national insurance plan, Social Security.

As Roosevelt set the goals for the nation's recovery he said, *"The only thing we have to fear is fear itself."* His "fireside chats" on the radio gave the people confidence.

America fought World War II while Roosevelt was President. He was an outstanding wartime leader. He met with Churchill and Stalin to make plans for victory. He believed the nations of the world must work together for lasting peace. He helped plan the United Nations.

Roosevelt died in 1945, just before the war ended. He was buried at Hyde Park. On his birthday many people send flowers to his grave.

His wife Eleanor carried on his work as a delegate to the United Nations. Many people called her the "First Lady of the World." Now she lies buried beside her husband. Visitors to Hyde Park can go through their home high above the Hudson River. The Roosevelts gave it to the nation.

One of the millions of men and women who helped Roosevelt win World War II was John Fitzgerald Kennedy. He was born in Brookline, Massachusetts, on May 29, 1917.

During World War II he commanded a PT boat in the Pacific Ocean. One night his boat was rammed by a Japanese destroyer. Two of his men were killed and Kennedy's back was severely injured. Even so he swam to an island. He helped save the other men in the crew and was given a medal for heroism.

After the war Kennedy went into politics. He served in both the House of Representatives and the Senate.

Once he had to have an operation on his back. He was in the hospital for a long time. While he was getting well he wrote a book called *Profiles in Courage*.

It was so good that it was awarded a Pulitzer Prize.

In 1961, Kennedy became the youngest President ever to be elected. His first speech as President stirred the whole nation. He said, *"My fellow Americans, ask not what your country can do for you; ask what you can do for your country."*

Kennedy's administration was called the New Frontier. It brought new hope and courage to many American citizens.

President Kennedy had some great ideas for keeping peace in the world and for helping people in other countries. Before many of these ideas could be carried out he was killed by an assassin. The date was November 22, 1963.

A few days later Kennedy was buried at Arlington National Cemetery.

Kennedy's grave is only a short walk from the spot where our unknown soldiers lie *"in honored glory."* It is just down the hill from the Custis-Lee mansion, Robert E. Lee's family home.

Arlington is a beautiful place. Across the Potomac River shines the nation's capital city which is a memorial to our first President. When Washington was alive he was too modest to call the city "Washington." He always spoke of it as "the Federal City."

From Arlington the great dome of the capitol building can be seen rising in the sky. George Washington laid the cornerstone for the capitol in 1793.

The Washington Monument and the Jefferson and Lincoln Memorials can also be seen from this hallowed ground. Memorials to Franklin D. Roosevelt and John F. Kennedy will soon be built near them.

The view from Arlington seems to link the lives of all our patriots. It is a sight that never fails to fill American hearts with pride.

Our history and heritage bind our country together, North with South and East with West. They make us:

"One nation under God, indivisible, with liberty and justice for all."